JULIAN EDELMAN

FLYING high 3

WITH ASSAF SWISSA

ILLUSTRATED BY DAVID LEONARD

Published by Superdigital, LLC
971 Commonwealth Avenue, Suite 32
Boston, MA 02215
www.superdigital.co

ISBN 978-0-578-58743-1

Printed in the United States of America
First Edition, 2019

Ordering Information
For wholesale orders by U.S. trade bookstores, corporations, associations and others, contact publishing@superdigital.co

Co-Written by Kyler Schelling
Produced by Billy Griffin

"Who is wise?
One who learns from all."
—Talmud

Jules is a squirrel that loves football.
He plays on a very good team.

After a long year, Jules and the team take a well-deserved summer vacation.

Everyone gathers at the beach.
Some animals like to surf waves
and some like to fly kites...

...some even
build sandcastles!

All of the animals are here
to play and have fun.

Jules is surprised to see someone
not playing with the others.

It's Tom the Goat!
"What's he doing?" Jules wonders.

He isn't playing at all. He's working to get better, even in the summer!

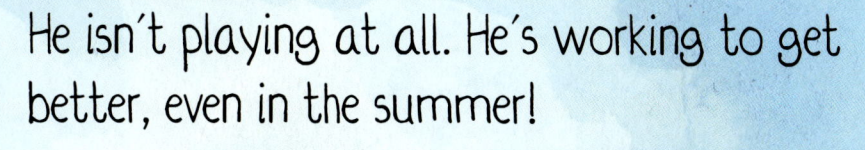

The next day, Jules wakes up early
and meets Tom at the beach.

They are ready to work.

He dashes through the cones
and catches Tom's pass.
Jules is doing great!

The Goat and the Squirrel work late into the night.

The next morning Jules is tired and sore.
"It's just the summer," he says.
"I'll get back to work tomorrow."

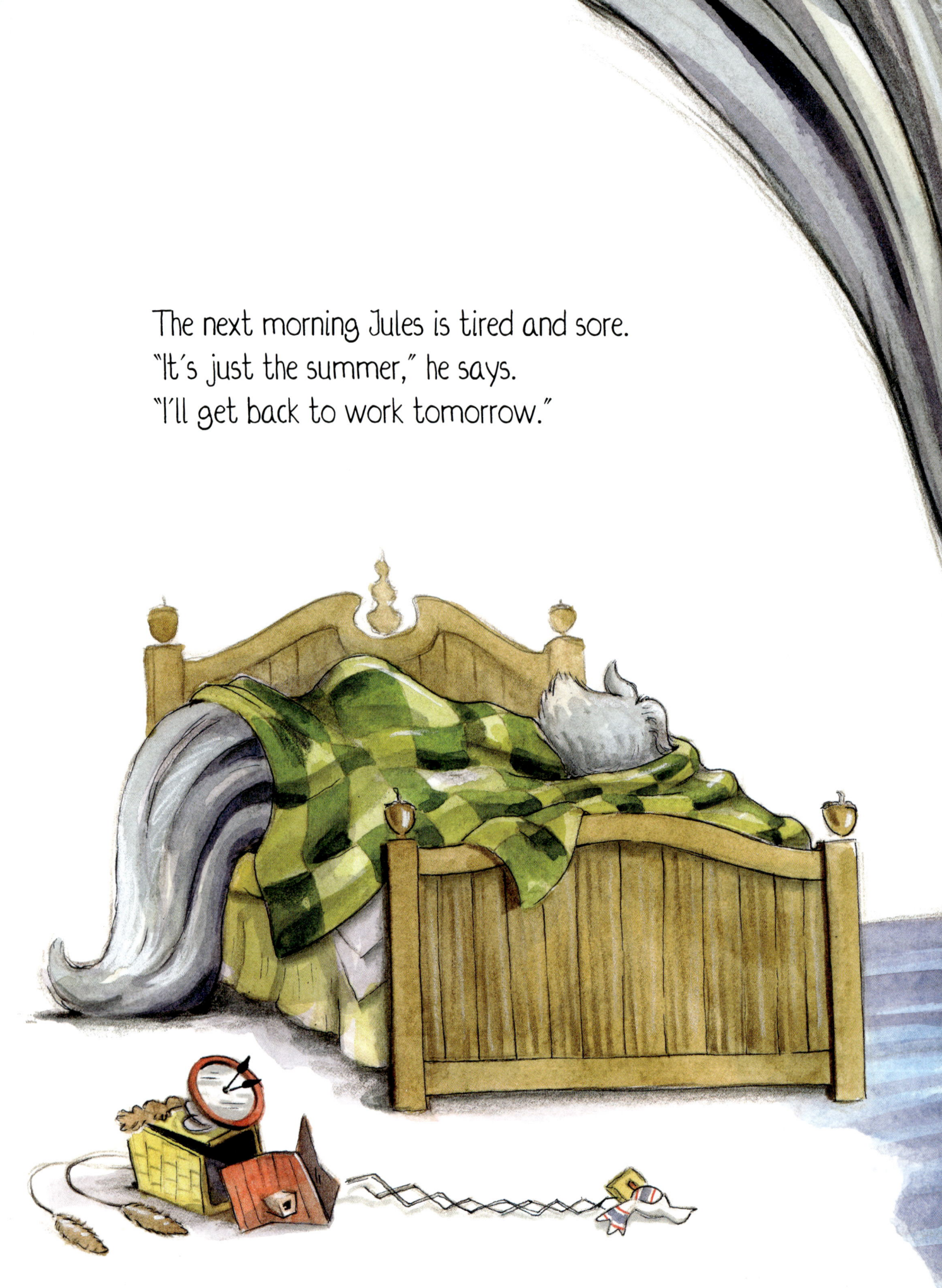

Jules joins the other animals to play and have fun.

He plays video games and eats his favorite foods.
Jules is enjoying the summer!

After his day of fun, Jules sees Tom walking back from his workout.

"You worked out today?" asks Jules.
"Yes," says Tom.
"But weren't you tired from yesterday?"
"Yes," says Tom.
"And you're going to workout tomorrow?"
"Yes," says Tom.

The next morning, Jules decides to wake up early.
He struggles to get out of bed.

Jules heads to the beach to workout with Tom.

He stumbles through the cones and drops Tom's pass.

Jules feels terrible.

"I'm so tired and sore," says Jules.
"Good," says Tom. "That's how you get better."

"We're not as BIG as the rhino,
as STRONG as the lion,
or as FAST as the eagle."

"Animals like us have to work hard
and we have to work hard every day."

Tom and Jules get back to work.
They train together the next day,
and the next day,
and the day after that...
all the way until the end of summer.

Jules is ready for football season!

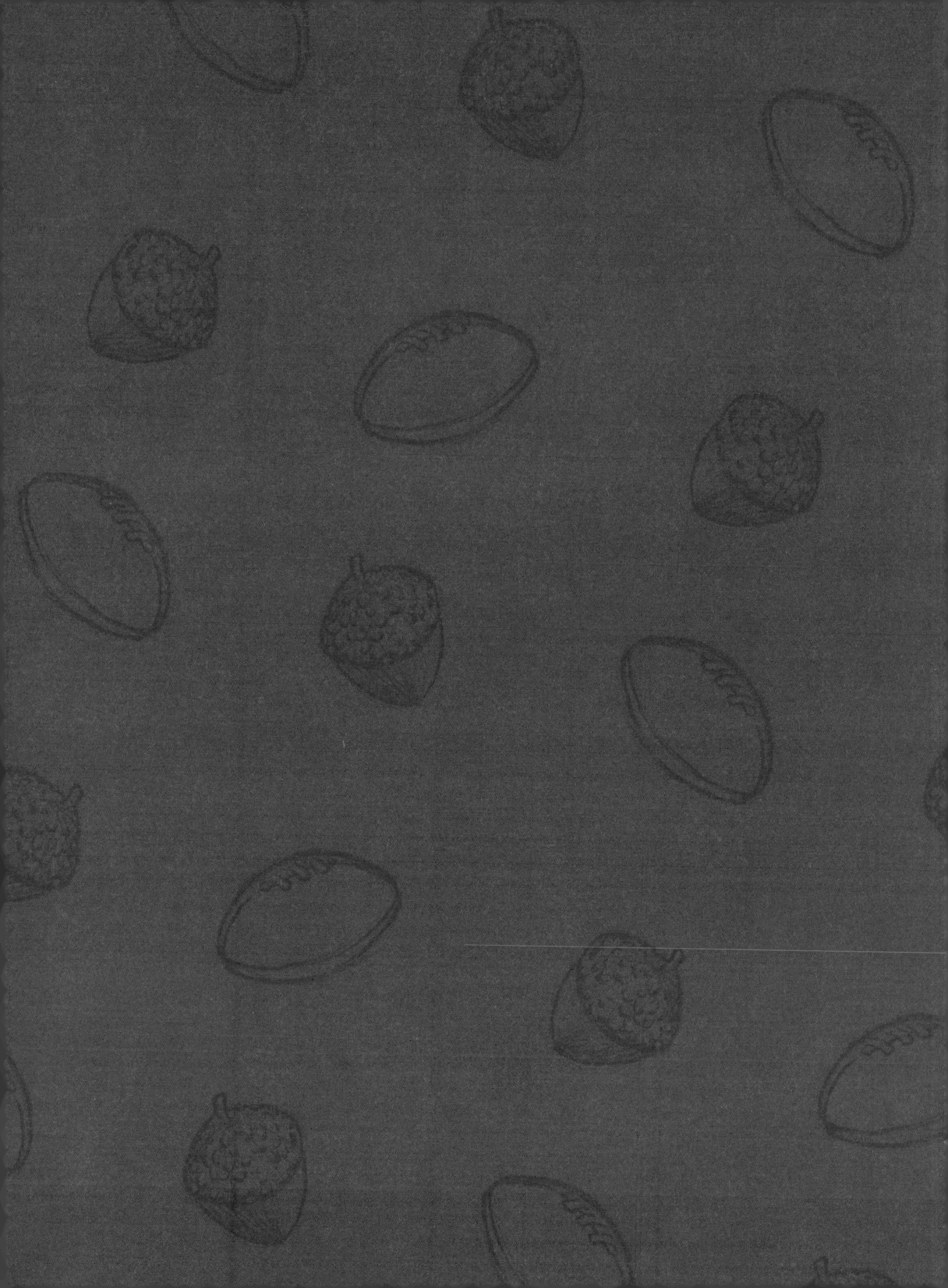